bean appétit

bean appétit

hip and healthy ways to have fun with food

SHANNON PAYETTE SEIP AND KELLY PARTHEN,
WITH CARISA DIXON

ILLUSTRATIONS BY RUSSELL DIETRICH

Andrews McMeel
Publishing, LLC
Kansas City · Sydney · London

09 10 11 12 13 CHO 10 9 8 7 6 5 4 3 2 1

ISBN-13: 978-0-7407-8517-7
ISBN-10: 0-7407-8517-6

Library of Congress Control Number: 2009923915

Illustrations by Russell Dietrich
Photographs on pages x, 118, and 148 by Nick Berard
Photographs on pages 58, 144, and 158 by Adeline Peck
All other photographs by Amy Lynn Schereck
Styling by Jessica Nordskog

Book design by Diane Marsh

www.andrewsmcmeel.com
www.beansproutscafe.com

ATTENTION: SCHOOLS AND BUSINESSES
Andrews McMeel books are available at quantity discounts with bulk purchase for educational, business, or sales promotional use. For information, please write to: Special Sales Department, Andrews McMeel Publishing, LLC, 1130 Walnut Street, Kansas City, Missouri 64106.

thanks to our peas corps:

Bean Sprouts Team

Bean Appétit Taste-Testers

Gale "VI-Pea" Gand

Judy "Grandma Bean" Seip

AND OUR SWEETEST PEAS:

Roger, Isaac, and Bini

Eric, Kale, and Makena

contents

CONTENTS

CONTENTS

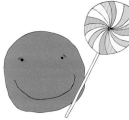

introduction

Welcome bitty bakers to *Bean Appétit*! This book's authors know oodles about kids and cooking. They are also the founders of Bean Sprouts—the nation's leading healthy kids' café and cooking school, where youngsters learn to create yummy, good-for-you recipes.

So, wash your hands and get ready to have a heap of food fun!

Look for these special sections and tips throughout *Bean Appétit*:

green bean
Recycle common
kitchen items
for eco-fun!

table talk
Quirky questions
to spark quality
conversations

pea brain
Fun food facts

refined bean
Tips for top table
manners

adult helper
Bitty bakers will
need some adult
assistance

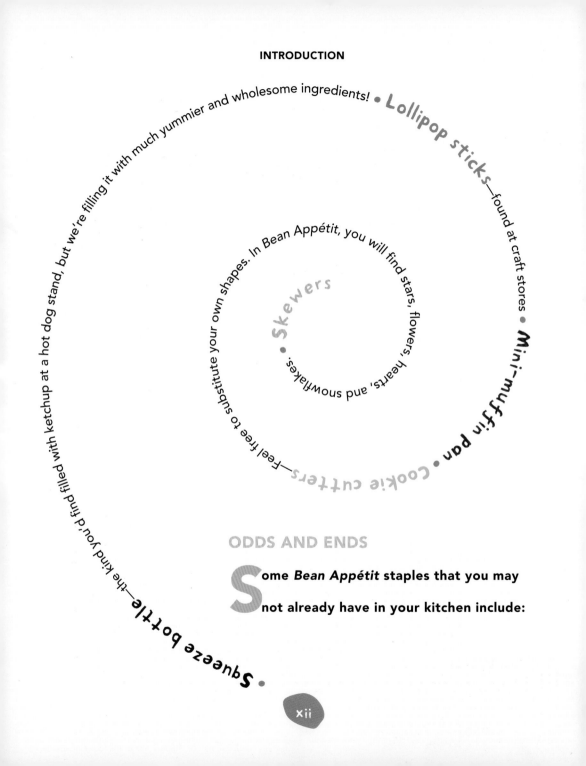

• **Lollipop sticks**—found at craft stores • **Mini-muffin pan** • **Cookie cutters**—Feel free to substitute your own shapes. In Bean Appétit, you will find stars, flowers, hearts, and snowflakes. • **Skewers** • **Squeeze bottle**—the kind you'd find filled with ketchup at a hot dog stand, but we're filling it with much yummier and wholesome ingredients!

ODDS AND ENDS

Some *Bean Appétit* staples that you may not already have in your kitchen include:

Save yourself from measuring cup madness! Prepare our Bean Appétit Flour Blend ahead of time, and you won't have to scramble to find the ingredients.

bean appétit flour blend

Combine the following ingredients and store in an airtight container:

3 cups whole wheat flour

3 cups unbleached all-purpose flour

2¼ cups wheat germ

½ cup flax meal

Finally, here's the trick on how to puree chickpeas, which we often use instead of butter in a recipe:

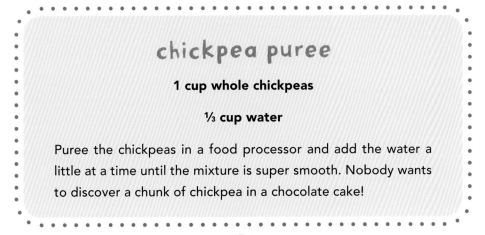

chickpea puree

1 cup whole chickpeas

⅓ cup water

Puree the chickpeas in a food processor and add the water a little at a time until the mixture is super smooth. Nobody wants to discover a chunk of chickpea in a chocolate cake!

become a star chef with our chef challenge!

Each chapter of *Bean Appétit* contains a different challenge—from cracking an egg to chomping with chopsticks. When you complete each challenge, cut out the matching square on page 193 and attach it to your *Bean Appétit* diploma, which you can download at www.beansproutscafe.com!

chickpea

RISE AND SHINE—
IT'S BREAKFAST TIME!

stick stacks

Makes 12 to 14 mini pancakes

1¾ **cups unbleached all-purpose flour**

3 **tablespoons packed light brown sugar**

1 **tablespoon baking powder**

2 **tablespoons flax meal**

Pinch of ground cinnamon

3 **eggs**

1 **teaspoon vanilla extract**

1 **tablespoon unsalted butter, softened**

1 **cup milk**

4 **strawberries, cut widthwise into thin slices**

2 **kiwis, peeled and sliced widthwise into circles**

¼ **cup blueberries**

Maple syrup, for serving

YOU WILL ALSO NEED:
   4 skewers

1. Chant "Pancakes! Pancakes!" as you combine the flour, brown sugar, baking powder, flax meal, and cinnamon.

2. Combine the eggs and vanilla in a mixing bowl. Add the butter and milk. Slowly add the egg mixture to the flour mixture. Stir until smooth. Chill in the freezer for 5 minutes.

3. Preheat a griddle to low. Lightly spray the griddle with nonstick spray. Ladle the pancake mixture onto the griddle to make 2-inch mini pancakes.

4. When the pancakes start to bubble lightly and the edges turn golden brown, flip them over. All bitty bakers should flip around the kitchen, as if *they* were just flipped with a spatula. Cook on the other side for 1 to 2 more minutes, until the pancakes come off the griddle easily with a spatula.

5. Layer the pancakes and fruit on the skewers. Dip in maple syrup and eat one layer at a time.

OVER EASY

Using construction paper, cut out 20 egg shapes. Flip through magazines and cut out 20 small pictures of objects, such as a kitten or kite. Paste an image on each egg.

Place your egg playing cards face down in a pile. Without looking at the picture, the first player draws an egg card and holds it over his head so that his opponents can see the image.

The first player can ask 10 questions to figure out what the object is. The opponents can only answer yes or no. If the player gets it right before asking all 10 questions, he earns a point. The player with the most points after 5 rounds wins!

SUNNY SIDE UP!

Start each morning with a smile. Before you eat a bite of breakfast, say something positive to your family, such as "Today is going to be the best day ever!"

pea brain

If you have a hard-boiled egg and a raw egg, it's easy to tell them apart without cracking them open. Just spin them. The one that spins longer is hard-boiled!

ready to roll-ups

Serves 4

PESTO

½ **cup packed spinach leaves**

Pinch of garlic powder

1½ **tablespoons shredded Parmesan cheese**

2 **tablespoons olive oil**

Pinch of salt and pepper

EGGS

8 **eggs**

⅓ **cup shredded cheddar cheese**

YOU WILL ALSO NEED:
Decorative toothpicks

1. Preheat the oven to 400°F.

2. Scrunch the spinach leaves, garlic powder, and Parmesan in a food processor. Before an adult turns it on, say, "¡Buenos días!" Slowly add the olive oil, and process until the pesto is thick and spreadable. Season with the salt and pepper, and, presto, you have pesto!

3. Crack the eggs and pour them into a mixing bowl without dropping any shells in the bowl. Use a fork to scramble them up.

4. Make a noise like an alarm clock as you lightly spray two 8 by 8-inch pans with nonstick spray. Pour half of the eggs into each pan.

5. Bake for 6 to 8 minutes, until thoroughly cooked. Top with the cheddar cheese and melt in the oven for an additional 2 to 4 minutes. Use a rubber spatula to slide the eggs out in one piece.

6. Use a butter knife to spread the pesto on top of the cheddar cheese. Carefully roll the egg up, then slice into 1-inch segments with a clean butter knife.

7. Stick a decorative toothpick into each egg roll-up. *Eggs*-tra helpings, please!

green bean

who's the toss?

You'll crack up over this *egg-straordinary* toss game!

YOU WILL NEED:

- Two cardboard egg cartons
- Paint
- Glitter, stickers, or other decorations
- Stapler
- Upright paper towel holder

Cut the bottom of each egg carton (the bumpy side) in half lengthwise, into strips of 6 eggcups. Paint and decorate with glitter, stickers, and so on. Let dry.

Staple the ends of one strip together to form a ring. Repeat with the other strips.

Place the paper towel holder on the floor. Stand back and try to toss the egg carton rings onto the paper towel holder. See how many you can get in a row!

Table talk

Would you rather swim in a river of maple syrup or sleep on a bed of humongous pancakes?

If you had to name your pet hamster after a cereal, what name would you choose?

If you could wake up in the morning and magically find yourself anywhere in the world for breakfast, where would it be?

FLIP-FLOP FLAPJACKS

Pretend an oatmeal container lid is a pancake. On one side write "me" and on the other side write "you."

In the morning, when you are trying to decide anything from what music to listen to on the ride to school, to who gets to crack the eggs for the pancakes, play Flip-Flop Flapjack.

Place the "pancake" on a spatula. Whoever is flipping the pancake is "me." Whatever side lands face up is the person who wins!

crack me up!

Crack an egg without the shell getting in the bowl. And if a little shell does fall in, use a larger piece of the broken shell to remove it. The shell magically acts as a magnet!

After completing the challenge, cut out the Chickpea square on page 193 and attach it to your *Bean Appétit* diploma!

let it bean

MAKE MUSIC
AND MUNCHIES!

dough-re-mi

Makes 12 notes

⅔ cup packed light brown sugar

5 tablespoons butter, softened

2 eggs

½ teaspoon vanilla extract

1¼ cups Bean Appétit Flour Blend (page xiii)

½ teaspoon baking soda

¼ teaspoon salt

2 tablespoons cocoa powder

⅛ teaspoon ground cinnamon, plus a pinch

Package of organic black licorice sticks

1. Preheat the oven to 350°F and lightly spray a baking sheet with nonstick spray.

2. Sing the song "Do-Re-Mi" as you mix the brown sugar and butter in a bowl. Add the eggs and vanilla. In another bowl, combine the Bean Appétit Flour Blend, baking soda, salt, cocoa powder, and cinnamon.

3. Let's get the two mixtures to sing in harmony. Add the dry blend to the butter mixture. Stir until the dough forms into a sticky ball. Chill for 1 hour. During this intermission, pick your favorite song and sing it in different styles—from opera and hip-hop to country and jazz!

4. Roll the dough into 1-inch balls and place on the prepared baking sheet. Bake for 8 to 10 minutes, until slightly firm.

5. Use the licorice to create 5 lines on a large plate. Place the cookies on the lines for musical notes. Use the licorice to make the note stems. *Fa-la-la!*

PB & JAMMIN'

Wiggle while you whisk with these tasty tunes!

- "Just a Spoonful of Sugar," from *Mary Poppins*
- "Banana Boat," by Harry Belafonte
- "Mashed Potato," by James Brown
- "Chicken Soup with Rice," by Carole King
- "Banana Pancakes," by Jack Johnson
- "Vegetables," by the Beach Boys
- "On the Good Ship Lollipop," by Shirley Temple
- "The Candy Man," by Sammy Davis, Jr.
- "Tea for Two," by Ella Fitzgerald
- "Yes, We Have No Bananas," by Billy Jones

string bean

KITCHEN KARAOKE

Together brainstorm 10 foods and 10 popular tunes everyone knows. Write them each on a separate piece of paper and put the food papers in one bowl and the tunes in another bowl.

Take turns picking a paper from each of the bowls. You have 1 minute to make up new lyrics featuring the food you chose. For example, if you chose "Twinkle, Twinkle, Little Star" and "Pear," your song might go something like this:

Twinkle, twinkle, little pear,

Why do you have purple hair?

Up above the world you fly

Like a hero in the sky.

Twinkle, twinkle, little pear,

Rescue me, I see a bear!

Sing your made-up song into a whisk or rolling pin "microphone"!

spice girl sprinkles

Clean out empty spice containers and peel off the labels. Fill with healthy alternatives such as wheat germ, cinnamon, and flax meal, and add a special treat, such as colorful sprinkles. Decorate with new labels and come up with silly spice names. Hippy, hippy, shake on oatmeal, applesauce, yogurt, and other favorite foods!

green bean

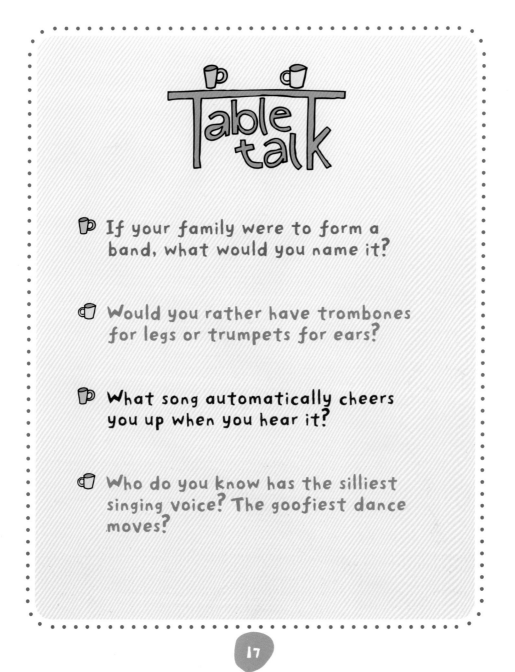

If your family were to form a band, what would you name it?

Would you rather have trombones for legs or trumpets for ears?

What song automatically cheers you up when you hear it?

Who do you know has the silliest singing voice? The goofiest dance moves?

17

high note nibbles

Serves 2

½   **cup plain yogurt**

1   **Granny Smith apple, cored and diced**

1   **tablespoon packed light brown sugar**

1½   **teaspoons lemon juice**

   Pinch of garlic powder

   Pinch of ground coriander

   Pinch of ground cinnamon

2   **tablespoons honey**

1½   **cups shredded rotisserie chicken**

1   **medium carrot, diced**

4   **slices whole wheat bread**

2   **slices rye bread**

1. Hum your favorite tune as you combine the yogurt, apple, brown sugar, lemon juice, garlic powder, coriander, and cinnamon in a mixing bowl. Add the honey, chicken, and carrot and mix well. Make 2 sandwiches on the whole wheat bread and 1 sandwich on the rye bread.

2. Cut the crusts off all the sandwiches, then cut the crustless whole wheat sandwiches into 1 by 2½-inch slices. Cut the crustless rye sandwich into ⅓ by 1¼-inch slices.

3. Arrange the "white keys" (whole wheat sandwich slices) side by side on a platter, and the "black keys" (rye sandwich slices) on top and in between the white keys to look like a piano keyboard. Pretend you're playing the keyboard in your favorite band before digging in!

19

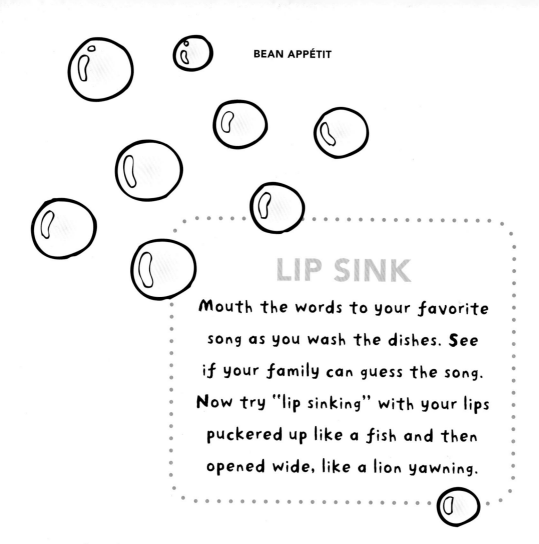

LIP SINK

Mouth the words to your favorite song as you wash the dishes. See if your family can guess the song. Now try "lip sinking" with your lips puckered up like a fish and then opened wide, like a lion yawning.

pea brain

The Vienna Vegetable Orchestra doesn't play instruments—they play veggies, including a pepper trumpet and a leek violin. At the end of each show, the audience gets a bowl of vegetable soup!

20

EDIBLE INSTRUMENTS

You can make your own percussion section with instruments you can eat!

ROCKIN' RATCHET

Cut the ends off of a carrot. Carefully cut triangle slivers all along the length of one side.

Use one sliver to strum back and forth!

BEAN-ANARAMA

Place ½ cup of dry beans in a travel mug and close the top. Shake!

CLIPPITY CLAPPER

Cut 2 slices in an eggplant lengthwise, stopping just short of the stem.

Hold the stem and wave the eggplant so the slices make a clapping sound.

RICE, RICE, BABY!

Place a cup of uncooked rice in a large metal bowl. Swish around to make a soothing snare drum sound.

Now rock out together to your favorite songs!

rock and roll-ing pin

Can you roll cookie dough without getting the dough stuck on the pin? Tip: Dust the rolling pin with flour or place it in the freezer for a few minutes!

After completing the challenge, cut out the Let It Bean square on page 193 and attach it to your *Bean Appétit* diploma!

beanbag

A TRIP TO
THE MARKET

BEAN-GO!

BEAN-GO!

Try new fruits and veggies with this tasty twist on bingo. Cross off each new food you taste until you get five in a row. Or play "blackout" (every square crossed out) for an even bigger reward of your choice!

Perplexed by purple cauliflower? Check out our Bean-Go! recipes at **beansproutscafe.com**!

(Turn the page to see the names of the foods.)

BEAN-GO

B E A N-GO

B	E	A	N-	GO
rutabaga	star fruit	rhubarb	fig	purple cauliflower
kale	pomegranate	quince	pluot	yellow bell pepper
sugar snap peas	bing cherries	asparagus	spaghetti squash	shiitake mushroom
cilantro	gooseberries	eggplant	parsnip	papaya
bok choy	plantain	green tomato	okra	lima beans

Congratulations! You just won a 5-minute supermarket shopping spree! What is the first item you put in your shopping cart?

How many grapes do you think would fit in a shopping bag?

If you were having a shopping cart race, would you rather be pushing the cart or sitting in the cart?

GREEN GOBBLER

Fill your plate with everything green at the market—from green spinach fettuccine topped with Creamy Green Sauce (recipe follows) to green grapes, broccoli florets, snap peas, and anything else that's green!

creamy green sauce

Serves 4

⅔   **cup lowfat cream cheese**

3   **tablespoons Pesto (page 7)**

⅔   **cup lowfat milk**

1.   Heat a small sauté pan over low heat.

2.   In a bowl, mix the cream cheese and pesto together until smooth. Slowly add the milk and mix really well. While you're mixing, take turns thinking of all the toys in your house that are green.

3.   Add the pesto mixture to the sauté pan. Heat the sauce until it starts to bubble, then stir it up.

4.   Mix 2 cups cooked pasta with the creamy green goodness. Sing any song with the word "green" in it, as you gobble your food down!

SUPERMARKET SCAVENGE

Take a different kind of list on your next trip to the market. Brainstorm a list together of people or things you might find, such as:

A veggie that starts with the same letter as your last name

A baby wearing an orange shirt

An item that costs $2.95

An employee named Ed

Five kinds of beans

See how many you can check off by the end of your shopping trip!

pea brain

In England and Australia, people call shopping carts "trolleys."

bag, you're it!

Decorate your reusable fabric shopping bags with colorful polka dots by using cans as stamps. Dip the bottom of the can into fabric paint and dot away!

green bean

the rainbow confection

Pick your favorite color of the rainbow. Plan a meal where each food is that color. We took the challenge ourselves and created the Green Gobbler (page 28)!

After completing the challenge, cut out the Beanbag square on page 193 and attach it to your *Bean Appétit* diploma!

beanpole

OUTDOOR EATS

campfire crunch

EACH CHEF NEEDS THE FOLLOWING INGREDIENTS:

3–4   **green grapes, sliced in half**

3–4   **red grapes, sliced in half**

1   **slice cheddar cheese**

2–3   **medium carrots, finely sliced**

6   **pretzel sticks, broken into pieces**

1. Clap your hands and rub them together to get them nice and warm. Place the grape halves, cut side down, in a small circle, about the size of a cup.

2. Use clean scissors or rip the cheddar cheese to look like flames. Gently press the cheese flames together so they stand up. Place them in the center of the grape fire pit. Lay the carrot pieces on the cheese, upright.

3. Place the pretzel pieces around the flames. Now sing a campfire song!

HAPPY TRAILS . . .

As you head out for a hike, shake up your snack mix with these 3-ingredient combinations!

dried apples + cinnamon graham sticks + **vanilla-covered raisins**

peanuts
+ dried banana chips
+ **carob chips**

PATRIOTIC PARTY

dried blueberries + dried cherries
+ frosted shredded wheat cereal

SUNSHINY DAY

dried pineapple + golden raisins + popcorn

everything's Rosy

strawberry-covered pretzels
+ dried strawberries
+ dried raspberries

bug bites

Makes 1 dragonfly sandwich

½   **whole wheat pita**

1   **baby dill pickle**

2   **thin carrot matchsticks**

¼   **cup lowfat cream cheese**

2   **tablespoons vanilla yogurt**

½   **teaspoon ground turmeric**

¼   **teaspoon garlic powder**

     Pinch of salt

2   **slices honey-baked turkey breast**

4   **thin orange slices**

4   **thin red apple slices**

YOU WILL ALSO NEED:
Clean scissors

1. Flap your arms 4 times. Now use clean children's scissors to cut the pita bread into four 1-inch ovals to help shape the wings. Use a butter knife to slice one-third of the pickle off the top and set aside for the dragonfly's head. The rest of the pickle will be its tail.

2. Use a toothpick to make 2 small holes on the top of the pickle head. Slide 1 small carrot stick into each of the holes for the antennae.

3. Buzz like a bug as you combine the cream cheese, yogurt, turmeric, garlic powder, and salt in a bowl. Spread it on top of your pita bread.

4. Place your turkey slices on top of each other and roll them up tightly. Place the turkey roll-up in the center of a plate. Place the pickle head at one end, and the rest of the pickle at the other.

5. To help our dragonfly fly, it needs wings. Place 2 pita ovals on each side of the turkey body. Stack the sliced oranges and sliced apples on the wings, making sure all tips are pointing in. Run around the house like you're a dragonfly whooshing through the air before landing at your lunch table for a scrumptious sandwich!

COMPASS AND GET IT!

Before you eat, search for your supper! Have a "hider" put your entrée, side dish, and drink in separate lunch boxes and hide the boxes around your yard. The hider has to give directions on how to get to each item, such as "Do 5 bear crawls toward the garden hose to find your corn on the cob!"

pea brain

Invite your friends over on August 10 to celebrate National S'mores Day with Go Bananas S'mores (page 43).

BAIT AND SWITCH

Each "fish" (player) fills a paper cup with 10 pieces of "bait" (Goldfish crackers). When you say "swim," the fish run to their bait and try to eat all the crackers with their hands behind their backs, trying not to let the crackers fall to the ground. Switch the bait to other snacks and hold another round. The winner is the fish that eats the most bait!

go bananas s'mores

Serves 4

1¼ **cups Bean Appétit Flour Blend (page xiii)**

½ **cup packed light brown sugar**

½ **teaspoon baking soda**

Pinch of ground cinnamon

3 **tablespoons butter, softened**

1 **tablespoon honey**

2 **tablespoons water**

1 **teaspoon vanilla extract**

¼ **cup chocolate chips, melted**

1 **large banana, peeled and cut into ¼-inch slices**

1. Preheat the oven to 350°F.

2. Sing the popular camp song "The Ants Go Marching" while combining the flour blend, brown sugar, baking soda, and cinnamon in a bowl. Add the butter and stir until combined. Add the honey, water, and vanilla and mix until the dough is sticky. Press the dough flat on a parchment-lined baking tray. Chill in the freezer for 5 minutes.

3. Pack the dough into a ball and roll it out on a lightly floured surface until the dough is about ¼ inch thick. Use your favorite cookie cutters to make at least 8 graham crackers. Poke holes all around the top of the crackers with a fork.

4. Bake for 12 to 15 minutes, until golden brown. Roll around like a banana on the floor while chanting "Go bananas!" Remove the graham crackers from the oven and let them cool.

5. Spread the melted chocolate on a graham cracker. Add a layer of banana slices on top. Top with another graham cracker. Do you want s'more? Make another batch!

 What kind of ghost story scares you the most?

Would you rather share your sleeping bag with a bat or a bear?

If you were going to hike the highest mountain, what would you want to be waiting for you at the top?

FLASH DANCE

Lighten the mood with this fun flashlight game!

Play this game when the sun goes down or in a dark room. Pick one person to be the flashlight holder. He must leave the group for a few seconds while everyone else picks the "dance leader" and forms a circle. The flashlight holder comes back to the center of the circle.

The dance leader's goal is to start a silly dance, such as the Mashed Potato, without letting on that she's the leader. The other dancers must copy her dance as she continues to switch moves. The flashlight holder must try and figure out who is the leader by shining his light on the dancers. Once he does, the dance leader becomes the flashlight holder.

can do!

Carefully open a can using a can opener. Be sure to recycle the can once it's empty!

After completing the challenge, cut out the Beanpole square on page 193 and attach it to your *Bean Appétit* diploma!

peacasso

CREATE A
MASTER-*PEAS*!

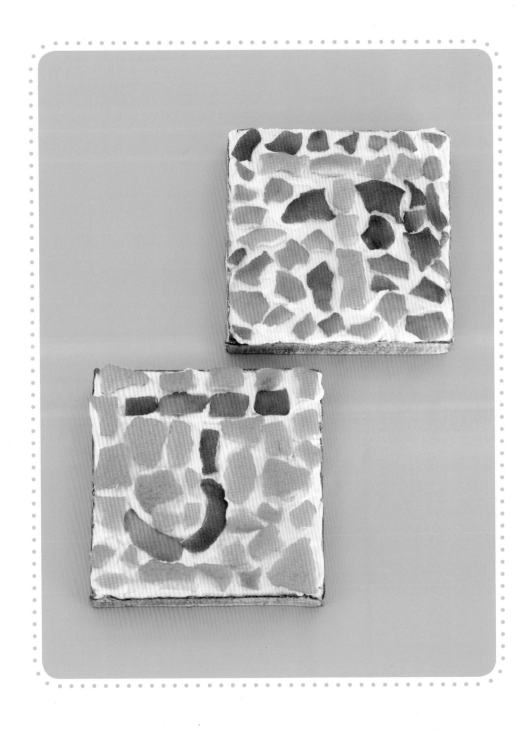

ZEST TO IMPRESS!

This citrus mosaic has mass ap-*peel*! Use bits of lemon, lime, or orange peels as your "tiles." Spread some cream cheese on a plate or other flat surface to serve as glue. Tear the peels into smaller pieces and place, color side up, in a creative design, or in your dinner guests' first initials for placeholders.

Table talk

- Which fruit or vegetable do you think is the hardest to draw?

- If you had to eat it when completed, would you rather make a sculpture out of cold scrambled eggs or cold oatmeal?

- How long do you think you could sit still for an artist to paint your picture? Ten seconds? Four minutes? Give it a try!

PALETTE FOR YOUR PALATE

Make a master-*peas* good enough to eat! Dab some colorful dips on pita bread to create your own edible paint palette (see below for ideas). Then use a clean plate or a dried lasagna noodle for the canvas. Experiment with fruits and veggies to serve as paintbrushes and stamps. Nibbling on art supplies is highly encouraged!

purple—boysenberry jam

yellow—honey mustard

orange—apricot puree

red—marinara sauce

green—pesto

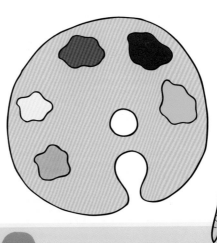

starry night bites

FOR EACH SKYSCAPE, YOU'LL NEED:

3   **tablespoons blueberries**

1   **tablespoon raspberries**

1½ **teaspoons packed light brown sugar**

1   **cup uncooked sticky rice**

1¼ **cups water**

½   **teaspoon dried thyme**

    Salt and pepper

2   **slices yellow cheddar cheese**

2   **slices Monterey Jack cheese**

YOU WILL ALSO NEED:
Moon and star cookie cutters

1. Combine the blueberries, raspberries, and brown sugar in a blender. Before an adult turns on the blender, say "Van GO!" Puree until smooth.

2. Rinse the rice and place it in a saucepan with the water, berry puree, and thyme. Bring to a simmer, then turn the heat to low and cover the pan with a lid. Cook the rice for 10 minutes. Turn the heat off and keep the lid on for 7 to 8 more minutes, until the rice is sticky and soft. Season with salt and pepper.

3. With great artistic flair, spread the rice on a plate, or your "canvas." Use a cookie cutter to cut star and moon shapes out of the cheese slices, and place them around the dark purple rice sky. Picture perfect!

MASHED MICHELANGELO

Choose one family member to pose like a statue. Use whatever ingredients you can—mashed potatoes, shredded wheat—to create a sculpture of that person. Take turns being the model.

pea brain

Some of the first paints were made with egg yolks, which would harden and stick to the surface.

COLOR ME YUMMY!

Which of the following is not the name of an actual Crayola crayon?

a. **Granny Smith Apple**

b. **Macaroni and Cheese**

c. **Shiitake Mushroom**

d. **Asparagus**

e. **Wild Strawberry**

Answer: c. Shiitake Mushroom

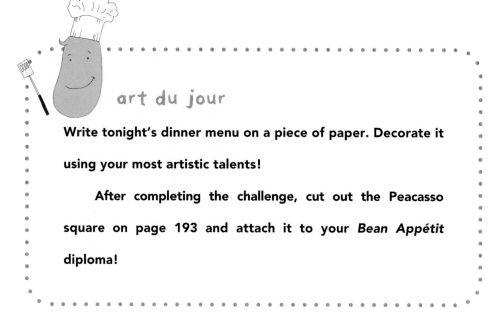

art du jour

Write tonight's dinner menu on a piece of paper. Decorate it using your most artistic talents!

After completing the challenge, cut out the Peacasso square on page 193 and attach it to your *Bean Appétit* diploma!

bean our guest!

A COOKING-THEMED
BIRTHDAY PARTY

HERE'S THE SCOOP

Invite guests to your cooking birthday party with utensil invitations. Use a permanent marker to write your important invitation information on the handles of sets of measuring spoons, including the who, what, when, and where. Hand out the invitations to guests and tell them to save up their appetites!

CHEF HAT SCAT

MAC

Prior to the party, come up with food pairs—salt and pepper, ice cream and cone—which will be used as chef names. You will need as many items as partygoers. Write one name on each chef hat (available at party stores, or make your own).

When birthday guests arrive, hand out hats name down, so they're a secret. When you say "Cooking time!" have them put on their hats and see who can find their food friend first!

CHEESE

super stars and salsa

EACH CHEF NEEDS THE FOLLOWING INGREDIENTS:

1   **whole wheat tortilla**

¼   **teaspoon ground cinnamon**

3   **tablespoons packed brown sugar, divided**

10   **red grapes**

10   **green grapes**

3   **strawberries**

1   **slice cantaloupe**

¼   **teaspoon vanilla extract**

YOU WILL ALSO NEED:
Star cookie cutters

1.   Preheat the oven to 350°F.

2.   Reach for the stars—a star cookie cutter, that is. Use the cookie cutter to cut shapes from the tortilla, and lay them on a greased baking sheet, making sure they don't overlap. Start shaking your hips as you mix the cinnamon and 2 tablespoons of the brown sugar together in a bowl and sprinkle it on the stars. Bake in the oven for 20 to 25 minutes, until they're light golden brown and slightly crispy. Let cool. While chips are in the oven, play Lickety-Split Oven Mitts (page 61).

3.   Use a butter knife to carefully cut the grapes in half, and the strawberries and cantaloupe into small pieces.

4.   Time to salsa dance! Combine the vanilla and the remaining 1 tablespoon brown sugar in a mixing bowl as you dance around the table, then add the fruit. Dip the sugary star chips in the salsa dip. Mmm . . . delish!

LICKETY-SPLIT OVEN MITTS

Everyone sits in a circle and puts on a pair of oven mitts (you may need to borrow some from friends). The object of the game is to work together to pass an item all the way around the circle.

Start with a bigger item such as a grapefruit. If anyone drops it, that becomes the new starting point to get it all the way around the circle. Once the item makes it around the circle, try a smaller object, then a smaller object, even one as tiny as a raisin!

READY, SPAGHETTI, GO!

Divide players into two teams. Place two large bowls filled with cooked spaghetti at the start line. Place two empty bowls across the room.

When you yell "Ready, spaghetti, go!," the first player from each team must use tongs to grab as much spaghetti as possible and carefully bring it across the room and dump it in the empty bowl. The players must run back to the start line and hand off the tongs to the next teammate.

Continue until every player gets a turn. The team with the most spaghetti in the second bowl is the *chomp*-ian!

pita boat pizza

EACH CHEF NEEDS THE FOLLOWING INGREDIENTS:

½   whole wheat pita pocket

½   cup shredded mozzarella cheese

2   tablespoons marinara sauce

¼   cup turkey pepperoni slices

10   sliced olives

2   teaspoons cream cheese, softened

1   carrot stick, about 5 inches long

1   thin cheese slice, cut into a triangle

YOU WILL ALSO NEED:
    1 small loaf pan per 2 bakers

1.   Preheat the oven to 400°F.

2.   Before you start cooking, everyone say in their best sailor voice, "Anchors Aweigh!"

3.   Open the pita pocket and place half of the mozzarella cheese in the bottom. Be sure to pack it in tight. Top with the marinara sauce, pepperoni, and the rest of the mozzarella cheese.

4.   Place your pita boat in the loaf pan so your boat is standing up. Place the loaf pans on a baking sheet lined with parchment paper, and write your name on the paper so you know which boat is yours.

5.   Bake for 6 to 8 minutes, until the mozzarella has melted. While the boats are baking, take turns pretending to walk the plank!

6.   After the boats are out of the oven, imagine you're the ocean breeze and blow on your boat for a few minutes to cool it off.

7.   Have an adult trim off a tiny bit of the rounded part of the pita at the bottom so you can stand your boat up.

8.   Lightly dip the olive slices into the cream cheese and place them on the sides of the pita for portholes. Press the carrot stick into the center of the pita for the mast. Attach the cheese triangle to the mast with the cream cheese. All hands on deck to enjoy!

WHY WHISK IT?

Choose a birthday guest to be the judge. Split the rest of the guests into three groups. Give each group a whisk. When the judge says "Go!" the group has 1 minute to come up with something besides mixing for which a whisk could be used. The answer could be as crazy as "an ear cleaner for a baboon." The judge decides which team has the best answer.

Let another birthday guest be the judge for the next round, and try other utensils, from a garlic press to a slotted spoon!

pea brain

As you celebrate your big day, can you and your birthday guests guess which of these celebrations is *not* an actual nationally recognized day?

a. Moldy Cheese Day

b. Sneak Some Zucchini on Your Neighbor's Porch Day

c. Pizza with the Works Except Anchovies Day

d. Peanut Butter Sandwich Without Crusts Day

e. Cry over Spilled Milk Day

Answer: d. Peanut Butter Sandwich Without Crusts Day

tricky taco shells

Makes 3 cookies per chef

EACH CHEF NEEDS THE FOLLOWING INGREDIENTS:

¼   **cup packed light brown sugar**

⅓   **cup whole wheat flour**

      Pinch of ground cinnamon

¼   **teaspoon vanilla extract**

1   **large egg**

1½   **teaspoons unsalted butter, softened**

YOU WILL ALSO NEED:
Aluminum foil

1. Preheat the oven to 375°F.

2. Shake your hips and get ready to mix! Stir the brown sugar, flour, and cinnamon in a bowl. Then whisk in the vanilla and egg. Mix lightly until smooth, then fold in the butter. Let chill for 5 minutes in the freezer.

3. Ladle the cookie dough into 3 circle shapes about 3 inches apart on a baking sheet lined with parchment paper.

4. Bake for 5 to 6 minutes, until golden brown.

5. While the cookies are baking, scrunch some aluminum foil into a log shape, about 12 inches long and 1 inch thick.

6. After the cookies have cooled for 1 minute, you must move fast! Have an adult help you drape a warm cookie over the foil log. Repeat with the remaining cookies. Once the cookies are cool, remove the foil carefully. You've just magically transformed the cookies into taco shells!

Turn the page to learn how to make the rest of your tricky taco treats!

sweet "meat" filling

EACH CHEF NEEDS THE FOLLOWING INGREDIENTS:

¼   **cup Bean Appétit Flour Blend (page xiii)**

1   **teaspoon cocoa powder**

2   **tablespoons packed light brown sugar**

¼   **teaspoon baking powder**

1   **tablespoon olive oil**

1   **teaspoon balsamic vinegar**

2   **tablespoons water**

2   **teaspoons milk**

1   **tablespoon chocolate chips**

1. Preheat the oven to 350°F.

2. Wink to each other, as if to let them in on the secret that you're about to trick someone. Combine the flour blend, cocoa powder, brown sugar, and baking powder in a mixing bowl. Then add the olive oil, vinegar, water, and milk and stir until combined. Fold in the chocolate chips.

3. Spray a mini muffin pan and pour in the cake batter. Bake for 10 to 12 minutes, until a toothpick inserted in the center of a cake comes out clean.

4. Even though you'll want to devour the cakes right away, let them cool enough so that you can break them up into small chunks to look like ground beef. Place the "meat" in the taco shells on page 64. Ask the person to your right, "Where's the beef?"

taco toppings

EACH CHEF NEEDS THE FOLLOWING INGREDIENTS:

1 **piece green fruit leather**

1 **slice peach**

1 **strawberry**

Rip the fruit leather into small strips and top your taco with "lettuce." Use a butter knife to cut the peach slice and strawberry into small pieces. Top your taco with your "cheese" and "tomato." Before tasting your tacos, shout whatever month it is (even if it's not April), then the word "Fools"—such as "February Fools!"

refined bean

Don't forget to send a thank-you note to each of your guests for coming to the party. Make sure to use the word "Chef" before your friend's name when addressing the envelope!

waterworks

Practice a steady pour! Have everyone stand in a line behind the birthday child with a 1-cup measuring cup (you may want to place a couple of beach towels on the floor to catch any drops). Fill the birthday kid's cup with water. She must pour the water into the next person's cup and so on. See how much water remains in the last cup. Try again to see if you can keep all the water in the cup!

After completing the challenge, cut out the Bean Our Guest! square on page 193 and attach it to your *Bean Appétit* diploma!

baked bean

**FOR A SIZZLIN'
SUMMER DAY**

sun-set your table with these signs of summer!

Eat off freshly washed Frisbees instead of plates.

Spread beach towels out in place of a tablecloth.

Serve lemonade out of a clean watering can.

BAKED BEAN

LEI IT ON ME!

Spruce up a simple salad with a small flower cookie cutter. Push the cookie cutter through your favorite ingredients—from pineapple slices to cucumber circles—to make flower shapes. Push a straw through the middle of each flower shape to make a hole. String all the ingredients onto a strand of rope licorice and tie the ends together. Put your lei on a bed of lettuce and drizzle with your favorite dressing. *Sun*-sational!

fla-mango soup

Serves 4

3   **ripe mangoes**

3   **tablespoons vanilla yogurt**

½   **cup pineapple juice**

2   **tablespoons water**

3   **large strawberries**

YOU WILL ALSO NEED:
Squeeze bottle

1. Peel, pit, and chop the mangoes.

2. Plop the mangoes, yogurt, and pineapple juice in a blender. Before an adult turns it on, yell, "Coconuts!" As the mixture whirls around, perform a quick hula dance.

3. Rinse the blender so it's clean. Combine the water and strawberries in the blender. Before an adult turns it on again, yell, "Surf's up!" and pretend you're surfing while the blender is on.

4. Blend until smooth, then pour the strawberry sauce into a squeeze bottle. Keep a steady hand while you draw a cool design or pattern on top of the soup. Hula-la!

look-alike lids

Easy to pack in your beach bag, this *lid*-tle game is big fun! Collect metal lids from frozen juice containers. Take matching pairs of stickers and put one on each lid (you need to make sure you have two of the same sticker). Lay the lids face down and play your homemade memory game.

green bean

TOP POPS!

Beat the heat with these healthy Popsicle combos. Have an adult blend the ingredients together, then pour the mixture into Popsicle molds and freeze overnight.

purple gurple
blueberries + raspberries + spinach + grape juice

peach bum
peaches + carrot juice + orange juice

night in guava-na
guava + applesauce + banana + pineapple juice

palm tree paradise

Serves 4

A taste of the tropics!

2	**teaspoons lime juice**
1	**teaspoon honey**
¼	**teaspoon ground cumin**
	Pinch of garlic powder
	Salt and pepper
2	**boneless, skinless chicken breasts**
1½	**cups water**
1	**pineapple, cut into 4 (1-inch thick) round slices**
¼	**cup cream cheese**
¼	**cup packed spinach leaves**
8	**dried figs**

YOU WILL ALSO NEED:
8 skewers

1. Preheat the oven to 400°F.

2. Pretend you're putting on sunscreen before you combine the lime juice, honey, cumin, garlic powder, and salt and pepper in a bowl. Place the chicken in a small baking dish. Pour the lime juice mixture all over the chicken, making sure the chicken is covered, then add the water to the baking dish. Place in the oven and bake for 18 to 20 minutes, until the chicken is thoroughly cooked. While the chicken is baking, pretend to dip your toes in the ocean!

3. Slice each chicken breast into 4 long pieces. Push a skewer lengthwise through each chicken piece to form tree trunks. There should be 8 chicken skewers.

4. Stick 2 chicken skewers into each pineapple slice. The pineapple is your island. Use the cream cheese to stick the spinach leaves onto the chicken tree trunks. Place 2 figs under the trees for coconuts!

HAVE A BALL!

Using a marker, write a silly action on each section of a beach ball, such as "Do the limbo!" During your summer picnic, take turns tossing the beach ball across the table to each other. You must do whatever action is facing you!

Esme's

pea brain

In some parts of the world, people don't shimmy up trees to collect coconuts, trained monkeys do!

Table talk

What one toy would you choose to bring with you to a deserted island?

If you could invite an ocean creature for lunch, would you rather invite an octopus or a dolphin?

Would you rather use a beach ball or a sand castle for a pillow?

MELTDOWN

Cleaning up after dinner has never been this n-*ice*! Put a small ice cube in a glass and challenge your family to clean everything before the ice melts. The hotter it is, the quicker you have to move! After your kitchen is spotless, you can all "chill out"!

scooper trooper

Practice using a measuring cup to scoop dirt or sand. Level off the top with a toy shovel. Once you can get the top nice and flat, use a clean cup to measure flour and a butter knife to scrape away the extra.

After completing the challenge, cut out the Baked Bean square on page 193 and attach it to your *Bean Appétit* diploma!

snow pea

**FOOD FUN FOR
A WINTRY DAY**

pear penguins

EACH CHEF WILL NEED:

2 **mini chocolate chips**

2 **white chocolate chips**

1 **pear**

3 **tablespoons chocolate chips, melted**

1 **thin slice of baby carrot, cut into a small triangle**

1 **fig, cut in half diagonally**

YOU WILL ALSO NEED:
Pastry brush

1. Your penguins need eyes to see how cute they will become! Push the mini chocolate chips in the center of the white chocolate chips to form eyes. Now waddle like a penguin twice around the table.

2. Even though penguins can't fly, they still need wings. Use a butter knife to carefully cut a slice in both sides of the pear to form wings, making sure to keep the tops of the slices attached to the pear. Use a peeler to shave the pear skin off in between the wings in an oval shape. This is the penguin's white tummy.

3. Use a pastry brush to paint chocolate on the penguin's body, everywhere but his stomach. Use a toothpick to notch a spot for each of the chocolate chip eyes and the carrot beak. Insert the eyes and carrot beak. Balance the pear penguin on a plate and place the fig halves for feet. Dress up in black and white clothes for this frosty feast!

snuggle-up soup and smitten-mitten sandwiches

Serves 4

SOUP

1   tablespoon olive oil

2   Granny Smith apples, peeled, cored, and diced

1   large sweet potato, peeled and diced

2   tablespoons packed light brown sugar

¼   teaspoon garlic powder

    Pinch of ground cinnamon

    Salt and pepper

⅔   cup water

4   whole Granny Smith apples

SANDWICHES

8   slices honey-roasted turkey

½   cup shredded Monterey Jack cheese

8   slices whole wheat bread

YOU WILL ALSO NEED:

Mitten cookie cutter
Melon baller

84

1. Preheat the oven to 350°F. Heat a sauté pan over medium heat and coat it with the olive oil. Sauté the diced apples until soft, 2 to 3 minutes. Add the sweet potato, brown sugar, garlic powder, and cinnamon and sauté for another 2 minutes. Season with salt and pepper. Add the water to the sweet potato–apple mixture and simmer until soft, about 6 minutes.

2. Who needs a bowl? We're going to use apples! While the sweet potato–apple mixture is cooking, slice the tops off the whole apples and set the tops aside.

3. Pretend it's a warm day at the beach, and you're scooping sand. Imagine a melon baller is your "shovel," and scoop the inside of each apple to form a bowl. But watch out! Make sure you don't scoop out the very bottom of the apple, or soup will ooze out everywhere. Set the apples aside.

4. To make the Smitten-Mitten Sandwiches, place 2 slices of turkey and a sprinkle of cheese on each of 4 slices of the bread. Place another slice of bread on top, and use a mitten cookie cutter to make mittens from each sandwich. Press the edges of the bread together to close them around the turkey and cheese, and place the mittens on a baking sheet.

5. Bake for 4 minutes, or until warm and yummy.

6. Wiggle your fingers to warm them up. Use a fork to smash the cooked sweet potato–apple mixture in a bowl, so it's nice and mushy. Taste and adjust the seasonings. Use a soup ladle to carefully pour the soup into your apples. Great job pouring! Place the apple lids on top for a perfect bowl of soup that will satisfy your *apple*-tite!

GETTING WARMER!

The first player closes his eyes and counts to 20. The rest of the family hides a small grape or a blueberry somewhere on the dinner table.

When the player is done counting, he must guess where the grape is. The others respond with "Cold" if he's far away, or "Warm" if he's getting close. If the answer is "Cold," the player needs to take a bite of his meal. When he eventually finds the grape, pick a new player and start over.

FAUX-BALL FIGHT

No snow? No problem! Fake it by taking old tights or socks and cutting them off at the ankles. Fill the feet with flour and tie off the tops. Head outside and throw your pretend snowballs. Make up your own games, such as faux-ball tag!

pea brain

The largest snowflake ever found was 15 inches across and 8 inches thick. That's bigger than your dinner plate!

87

Table talk

What is the silliest way you could dress a snowman?

If snow had to be a color other than white, which color would you choose? Why?

Would you rather sled down a slope of pasta or mozzarella cheese?

POLITE BY CANDLELIGHT

Warm up your family dinner with candlelight. Take a vote on who had the best manners throughout the evening. That person gets to blow out the candle!

refined bean

whip it good!

Use a hand mixer to make your own whipped cream for hot cocoa! Add 1 teaspoon of vanilla extract and 1 tablespoon of confectioners' sugar to 1 cup of heavy cream. Hold the mixer tight and whip the mixture on medium-high speed until the cream is light and fluffy!

After completing the challenge, cut out the Snow Pea square on page 193 and attach it to your *Bean Appétit* diploma!

world peas

AROUND THE GLOBE
WE GO!

mama mato!

Makes 2 faces

1   **medium tomato, cut in half**

6   **tablespoons bread crumbs**

5   **tablespoons shredded Parmesan cheese**

     Pinch of garlic powder

2   **slices black olive**

4   **ounces spaghetti, cooked**

2   **basil leaves**

1.   Preheat the oven to 400°F.

2.   Ready to scoop? Use your spoon to dig out the goopy center of each tomato half.

3.   In a mixing bowl, combine the bread crumbs, 2 tablespoons of the Parmesan, and the garlic powder. How does it smell? Give it a whiff! Fill the holes in the tomato halves with the garlicky mixture. Top the tomato halves with the rest of the Parmesan.

4.   Use a butter knife to cut the olive slices in half. Place 2 slices on top of each tomato half for eyes. Place the tomato halves on a baking sheet.

5.   Mama Mato now needs a great hairstyle! Place the cooked pasta on the baking sheet in whatever style you'd like—curlicues, long and straight, or short and sassy. (You'll put the hair on her head after it comes out of the oven.) Kiss the tips of your fingers and say, "Ciao, Mama Mato!" before putting the pan in the oven.

6.   Bake Mama Mato for 8 to 12 minutes. While it's baking, see if you can style your hair like Mama Mato's.

7.   Transfer the tomato halves to a plate to cool for a few minutes. Tear the top of each basil leaf off and place it under the eyes for a smile. Now add the spaghetti hair to the tomato top to create a super style.

PLACE MAP PERSONALITIES

Each person secretly picks a country and draws its flag on a piece of construction paper to make a "place map." Turn over your place map and put it face down at a seat at your dining table.

Choose a place to sit, but not at the seat where your place map is. Flip over your new place map to reveal the country. Make up a new name for yourself and take turns sharing a story of what you did that day in your country. What games did you play? What did you learn at school? What did you eat for breakfast?

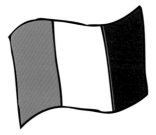

TORTELLINI TEST

See if you can match the type of pasta to what its name means in Italian!

1. spaghetti

a. bells

2. farfalle

b. pens

3. penne

c. twine

4. campanelle

d. boiling pot

5. lasagna

e. butterflies

pot sticker pinwheels

Serves 4

¼ cup honey

1 tablespoon Dijon mustard

2¼ cups diced cooked chicken

1 medium carrot, diced

1 medium zucchini, diced

¼ teaspoon salt

24 round pot sticker wrappers

2 ripe avocados, peeled
and pitted

Pinch of ground cumin powder

Juice of ¼ lime

¾ teaspoon garlic powder

2 medium carrots,
steamed and pureed

½ cup edamame, cooked

1. Preheat the oven to 375°F.

2. Spin in a circle three times before making your pinwheel filling. Now combine the honey, mustard, chicken, carrot, zucchini, and salt in a bowl.

3. Place a spoonful of the mixture in the center of each pot sticker wrapper. Fold in half and pinch the sides shut. Place on a baking tray and bake for 5 to 7 minutes, until lightly golden brown around the edges. Let cool slightly by blowing on the pot stickers, just as you blow on a pinwheel.

4. In a food processor, combine the avocados, cumin, lime juice, and garlic powder. Puree until smooth.

5. Dip the rounded edges of 12 of the pot stickers in the avocado puree and the other half of the pot stickers in the carrot puree.

6. Spin two more times before putting your pinwheel together. Place 6 pot stickers in a circle, alternating colors. Use the edamame to make a stick for the pinwheel.

India: pickled ginger

Brazil: green peas

Costa Rica: coconut

Japan: eel

Australia: shrimp and pineapple

TASTY TOPPINGS

What's your favorite pizza topping? **Here are some kids' favorites in other** parts of the world:

CRACKER COUNTRIES

Open a box of your favorite rectangular crackers, such as graham or club crackers. Use slices of cheese; fruit leather; blueberries; sliced olives; or anything else in your kitchen to create the flags of different countries. Here are some flags to try. Get creative!

Tanzania

Pakistan

Thailand

Switzerland

Canada

refined bean

TABLE MANNERS
FROM OTHER COUNTRIES!

Wipe your mouth with your napkin after every sip you take in Brazil.

Slurp your noodles as loud as you can in Japan. It means they're so delicious that you want to eat them as fast as possible!

It's considered respectful in Ethiopia to scoop up food (with your *injera* pancake) and gently feed it to your family member using your fingers.

In India, wait until the oldest person has started eating before you eat.

Birthdays are slippery in Canada, where friends grease your nose with butter for luck!

In many Latin American countries like Panama, kids try to whack down a piñata so the candy and prizes inside come spilling out.

In Brazil, birthday guests get veggies instead of cake!

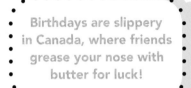

No birthday cake in Russia, either. There, they celebrate with birthday pies!

When you turn 5, 10, 15, or 20 in Holland, you get to wear a special crown!

If it's your birthday in the Philippines, your family decorates the outside of your house with blinking colored lights!

In Israel, the birthday child sits in a chair decorated with streamers and guests dance around in a circle.

Birthday kids in Australia eat a treat called fairy bread!

birthday traditions from far and wide!

petite piñatas

Make the **baked star cinnamon chips** through step 2 on page 60. Cut ½-inch-wide strips of different colored **fruit leather**. Cut little notches along the long sides of the fruit leather strips to make fringe. Layer the fringe on top of the star cinnamon chips, then trim away any excess leather along the edges of the chips so that it's in a star shape. No need to hit the piñata, just gobble it down!

STICK IN THE MUD

Clean your disposable chopsticks after you've eaten Asian food. Let dry. Tie colorful ribbons on the tops of the chopsticks. Use a fun tag (available at craft stores) to label an herb or a plant you're growing in your garden. Tie the tag to the ribbon and stick the chopstick plant marker in the pot!

pea brain

French toast was once called "poor knight's pudding" because it was made with old stale bread and crusts!

the chopstick chomp

Use a pair of chopsticks to pick up a piece of food (like the pot stickers you made on page 96) and feed it to someone else. If you can do it three times, you win the challenge!

After completing the challenge, cut out the World Peas square on page 193 and attach it to your *Bean Appétit* diploma!

104

balance beans

STACK AND SNACK!

THE LEANING TOWER
OF PEA-SA

P ut on your hard hat! To build your *master*-peas, you'll need dried pasta (any kind will do), cooked peas and carrots, and a plate. Using your plate as a foundation, stick your pasta, peas, and carrots together to construct any sort of building you can imagine. Try making a replica of the Eiffel Tower, the Great Pyramids, or the Golden Gate Bridge!

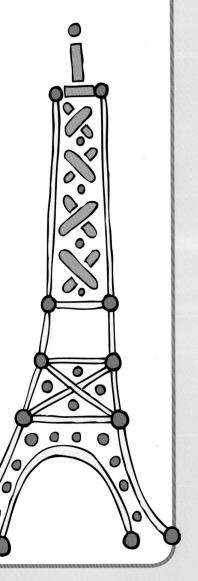

HOUSE OF CHARDS

Who needs a bowl when you can make your
own salad stacks? Skewer your favorite
veggies and salad greens on a stick
and drizzle with dressing.

pea brain

The tallest sandwich ever
made was 50 feet tall. That's
as high as a 5-story building!

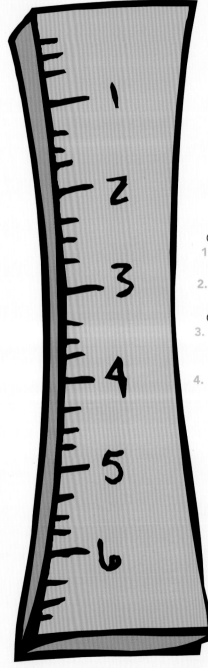

taco tower

Have you ever made your own tortilla chips before? It's easy!

1. Preheat the oven to 350°F.

2. Use a pizza cutter or clean children's scissors to cut each corn tortilla into 4 big chips.

3. Place the chips on a baking tray and bake for 12 to 15 minutes, until crispy.

4. Stand on your tiptoes as you place 1 chip on a plate and add a thin layer of each of your favorite taco fillings, such as ground turkey, shredded cheese, olives, tomatoes, and guacamole. Step on a phone book and stack another chip on top, followed by another layer of each filling. Repeat until your taco tower is super tall and so are you!

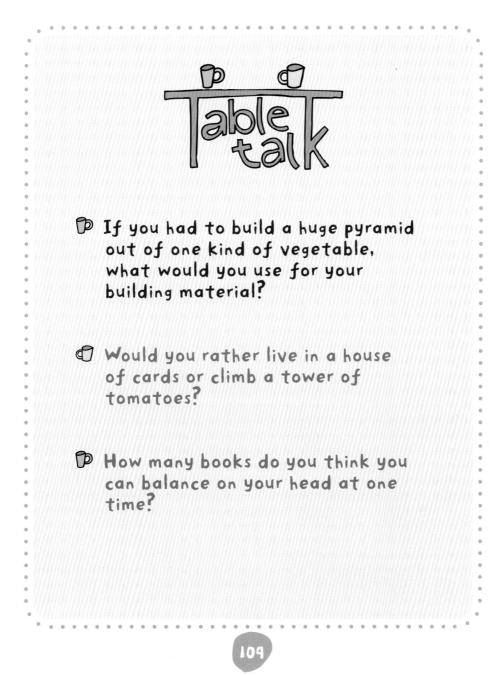

If you had to build a huge pyramid out of one kind of vegetable, what would you use for your building material?

Would you rather live in a house of cards or climb a tower of tomatoes?

How many books do you think you can balance on your head at one time?

STACK 'N' SIP

Make 3 different colored smoothies. Pour one color in the bottom of a glass. Layer the second smoothie on top. Add a top layer using the final smoothie. It's a triple-decker drink!

110

breakfast
bunker

Collect empty cereal boxes
(and get your friends to do the
same) until you have enough to build a fort.
Construct it with duct tape, and decorate
it with your own artwork!

green bean

CRACKER STACKERS

Place a paper plate on top of your head. Have someone place a cracker on top of your plate. Walk around the table while balancing the plate on your head. Don't let the cracker fall off.

Keep adding more crackers and see how many you can balance!

112

multi-decker dessert!

Make eight 6-inch **pancakes** using the recipe on page 2. The first family member places 1 pancake on a plate, then adds a layer of his favorite topping, such as **Nutella**, **strawberry jam**, or **peanut butter**. He passes the plate to the next family member, who tops that with another pancake and her favorite topping. Repeat until all the pancakes are used and your cake is stacked high. Cut the cake into slices and serve.

shredding bliss

Practice using a cheese grater. Decide if you want cheese shredded, sliced, or finely grated. Be careful not to get your fingers too close! You can add your finished work to the Taco Tower on page 108!

After completing the challenge, cut out the Balance Beans square on page 193 and attach it to your *Bean Appétit* diploma!

pea party

TIME FOR A
TINY TEA PARTY!

ITSY INVITES

Invite your friends to your tiny tea party with an itty-bitty invitation.

Write the details of the party on a long thin strip of paper, roll it up, and secure it with a little rubber band. Place the paper in an empty matchbox. Fill the matchbox with yummy-smelling tea leaves. Wrap the matchbox in cute paper and tie with a bitty bow.

Time for a tea party! At Kate's h

T TIME!

nstead of your real name, choose a name that starts with the letter T, such as Tallulah, Theodore, or Tessa!

pea brain

The biggest tea party was in India, with more than 30,000 people sipping their tea at the same time!

117

bitty baskets

Makes 4 baskets

¼ **cup honey**

3 **tablespoons peanut butter**

3 **tablespoons packed light brown sugar**

2 **teaspoons water**

¼ **cup crispy rice cereal**

2 **tablespoons old-fashioned oats**

¼ **teaspoon flax meal**

1 **tablespoon wheat germ**

¼ **cup fresh raspberries**

¼ **cup whipped cream**

YOU WILL ALSO NEED:
Mini muffin pan

1. Daintily place the honey, peanut butter, brown sugar, and water in a microwave-safe dish. Heat it in the microwave for 45 seconds and let sit for 1 minute. Stir the ingredients until smooth.

2. In a different bowl and with pinky raised, combine the rice cereal, oats, flax meal, and wheat germ. Mix the honey ingredients with the cereal ingredients until the mixture feels like Play-Doh.

3. Spray a mini muffin pan with cooking spray. Take a little ball of the dough and push it up the sides of each muffin cup to form a little basket. Dab your forehead with a hanky if this gets too tiring. Place the pan in the freezer for 30 minutes.

4. Carefully remove each basket and fill it with raspberries, then top it with a dollop of whipped cream.

5. Before you eat your first course, you must all curtsy!

PROPER PINKIES

At your tea party, tell everyone to raise their pinkies while drinking tea. If you catch someone not raising her pinky, you get a point. Whoever has the most points at the end of the party wins!

refined bean

In the Victorian era, it was proper to drink tea with your pinky lifted. That's because teacups were made without handles, and a raised pinky helped to balance the cup.

Take turns answering these questions at your tea party!

If you had to be ultra proper for the entire day, how long do you think you could go without getting your white gloves dirty?

Would you rather wear a tiara or a feather boa to a tea party?

If you had to change your name to the name of a tea, would you choose Oolong, Chamomile, or Ceylon?

sweetheart sandwiches

Serves 4

2   small sweet potatoes, peeled and sliced into 16 (¼-inch-thick) circles

Olive oil, for brushing

1   tablespoon packed light brown sugar

Pinch of salt

8   slices honey-baked turkey breast

¼   cup organic cranberry sauce

½   cup dried cranberries

YOU WILL ALSO NEED
Heart-shaped cookie cutter

1.   Preheat the oven to 375°F.

2.   Wear your heart—or at least heart-shaped stickers— on your sleeve as you use small heart-shaped cookie cutters to cut 16 hearts from the sweet potato slices. Place the potato hearts on a baking tray and lightly brush them with olive oil. Sprinkle with the brown sugar and season with a pinch of salt.

3.   Bake in the oven for 5 to 6 minutes, until the potatoes are slightly soft.

4.   Take turns listing something you love as you use heart-shaped cookie cutters to cut shapes from the turkey slices. Place 1 sweet potato heart on a plate. Stack with 2 turkey heart slices, spread with ½ tablespoon of cranberry sauce, and top with a few dried cranberries. Place your last sweet potato heart on top to finish off your sandwich. Place 2 cranberries in a heart shape on top of the sweet potato. Repeat until you've made all the sandwiches.

5.   Before you eat your second course, all guests must say "Fabulous!" with their best English accent!

third course
lollipop cakes

Serves 4

Make the cake recipe used for the Sweet "Meat" Filling on page 66

YOU WILL ALSO NEED:

3–4   tablespoons milk

4   lollipop sticks

½   cup chocolate semisweet chips, melted

        Cake sprinkles

1. Don't dismay! This step is a little strange. When your cake is cooled, mash it up into pieces in a bowl. Add the milk until the cake becomes sticky.

2. Form 1-inch-diameter balls using the sticky cake. Carefully slide a lollipop stick in each ball. Place in the freezer for 20 minutes, or until the cake hardens.

3. Dip each cake ball in the melted chocolate and decorate it with sprinkles. Set the cake balls on parchment paper and let them cool for 10 minutes, or until the chocolate is hard.

4. Before you eat your third course, you must air-kiss each other on both cheeks!

GLAD HATTER

Take turns passing around a fancy hat. When it's your turn, place the hat on your head. Pantomime something that makes you glad—from your new puppy to scoring a goal. Without saying any words, use your body language to give clues and see if the group can guess!

tea tipper

Pour your tea without spilling a single drop! After completing the challenge, cut out the Pea Party square on page 193 and attach it to your *Bean Appétit* diploma!

LIBERTY

IN BEAN
WE TRUST

2007

susan bean anthony

MAKE MONEY WITH
YOUR TASTY TREATS!

ONE-STOP SHOP!

Find friends with other talents—buddies who can offer additional services at your lemonade stand. That way you can draw more people in with your lemonade and offerings such as:

• dog petting • joke telling • stroller cleaning • mini-manicures

awesome ades

Give your lemonade stand extra pizzazz!

Start with blending the following ingredients of this basic lemonade recipe:

6 cups water

2 cups organic lemon juice

1 cup sugar

THEN STIR IN ONE OF THESE TASTY TWISTS:

Parched Piña—4 cups pineapple juice

Who's Your Papaya?—1 papaya, juiced in a juicer

Tangy Mango—1 mango, juiced in a juicer

Just blend the ingredients in a pitcher, chill, and start serving!

PUCKER UP!

For an extra 25 cents, ask your customers to play Pucker Up.

Before you open your lemonade stand in the morning, scoop out the insides of 3 lemon halves. Place a grape under one of the halves on your lemonade stand in front of your customers. Tell customers to keep their eyes on the lemon that's hiding the grape. Without lifting the halves, rotate the lemons as quickly as you can for about 30 seconds.

Can they guess which lemon has the grape? If they win, give them a free refill of lemonade!

BITES IN A BOX

hese colorful cooking mixes are a top seller!

Purchase colorful take-out containers at a craft store. Place the dry ingredients of one of the recipes on the following pages in a resealable plastic zipper bag. Seal the bag and place it in the container. Also place a small sheet with directions inside the box.

Write the name of the recipe, the price, and your name on a tag and stick it on the top of the take-out container. Create a couple of different versions, so your customers have a variety of choices!

cinnamon-oat pancake mix

Makes 10 pancakes

ADD TO THE PLASTIC BAG:

½   **cup Bean Appétit Flour Blend (page xiii)**

¼   **cup quick oats**

2   **tablespoons packed brown sugar**

1½   **teaspoons baking powder**

¼   **teaspoon ground cinnamon**

INCLUDE THESE DIRECTIONS FOR THE CUSTOMER:
Combine 3 eggs, 1 teaspoon vanilla extract, 2 tablespoons softened butter, and 1 cup milk. Slowly add the Cinnamon-Oat Pancake Mix. Stir until smooth. Preheat a griddle to low. Lighly spray the griddle with cooking spray. Ladle the pancake mixture onto the griddle to make the pancakes. When the pancakes start to bubble lightly and turn golden brown, flip them over. Cook on the other side for 1 to 2 more minutes, until the pancakes come off the griddle easily with a spatula.

pumpkin cranberry muffin mix

Makes 12 muffins

ADD TO THE PLASTIC BAG:

¾ **cup Bean Appétit Flour Blend (page xiii)**

½ **teaspoon ground cinnamon**

½ **teaspoon ground nutmeg**

¼ **teaspoon ground allspice**

½ **teaspoon baking soda**

⅛ **teaspoon salt**

⅔ **cup packed brown sugar**

⅓ **cup dried cranberries**

INCLUDE THESE DIRECTIONS FOR THE CUSTOMER:

Preheat the oven to 350°F. Beat together 6 tablespoons canned pumpkin, ¼ cup olive oil, 1 large egg, and 2 tablespoons orange juice until blended. Add the Pumpkin Cranberry Muffin Mix and stir until just moistened. Pour the batter two-thirds full into a greased muffin pan. Bake for 20 to 25 minutes, until a toothpick inserted into the center of a muffin comes out clean.

More recipes are available on our Web site at www.beansproutscafe.com.

pizza portraits

These personalized pizzas will bring you big bucks!

Let your neighbors know that you'll be delivering pizza portraits on Saturday (or whatever day you choose) for a set price. Tell them you'll handcraft a pizza that looks like their face!

Make sure to take a notebook to ask your neighbors which pizza toppings they do and do not like.

1. Use a **whole wheat pita** as a crust. Add **sauce** and place toppings such as **turkey pepperoni**, **sliced olives**, **sliced tomatoes**, **broccoli**, and **cheese** on top of the pita to create a pizza that looks like your neighbor's face.

2. Bake in a preheated oven at 400°F for 8 to 10 minutes, until the cheese is melted and golden.

3. Place on a plate and cover carefully with foil so as not to mess up the face. Deliver immediately!

refined bean

Set your selling off on the right note by greeting your customers with a smile. And always thank them, even if they don't buy anything!

green bean

herb-an legend

Use your green thumb to earn extra dollars! Tell your customers you can plant herbs for them in personalized pots. Paint and decorate empty large yogurt or cottage cheese containers. Plant seeds in your pots and tend until the plants are little seedlings. Add a name stick from page 103 for an extra touch. They're ready to sell!

MS. HEWITT

136

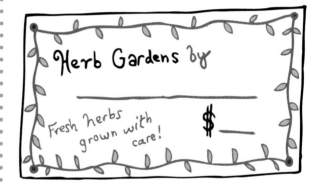

BIZ KID

Fill in your info on these business cards, then make copies and hand them out to customers!

Bites IN A Box

by
_____

Easy to make!
mmmm!

$ ☐

Herb Gardens by

_____

Fresh herbs grown with care!

$ ___

_____'s Personalized Pizzas

Yummy & Good-for-you!

$ ___

squeeze play

Squeeze 2 lemon halves to get all the juice out. It helps to press down on and roll the whole lemon on a table or work surface to get it soft and juicier before you cut and squeeze it.

After completing the challenge, cut out the Susan Bean Anthony square on page 193 and attach it to your *Bean Appétit* diploma!

peanocchio

BOOK-THEMED

FOOD AND FUN

the very hungry caterpillar

Based on the book by Eric Carle

EACH CHEF WILL NEED:

½   **avocado, peeled, pitted, and thinly sliced**

1½   **teaspoons packed light brown sugar**

1   **tablespoon light coconut milk**

2   **tablespoons diced mango**

¼   **cup shredded rotisserie chicken**

½   **teaspoon lime juice**

1   **tablespoon light soy sauce**

1   **(6-inch) piece rice paper (available at Asian food stores)**

      Pretzel sticks

1   **plum tomato**

2   **dried currants**

2   **thin carrot matchsticks**

1. Wiggle while you combine the avocado, brown sugar, coconut milk, mango, chicken, lime juice, and soy sauce in a mixing bowl. Let sit for 5 minutes. (You can stop wiggling now!)

2. This step is like magic. Fill another bowl with warm water and place the rice paper in the bowl. Wave your hands over the bowl like a magician and shout, "Abra-cadabra!" Let it sit until the rice paper is soft and almost invisible! Remove the rice paper from the water. Let it sit on a clean plate for 1 minute. Don't worry—it should be kind of sticky.

3. Place the avocado mixture on the lower center of the rice paper. Fold the outside in so it touches and roll the bottom of the paper up to form a log shape. Carefully slice the log into 5 equal pieces. This is the caterpillar's body. Place pretzel sticks around the body for legs.

140

4. To make the caterpillar's head, carefully slice off one-third of the tomato. This piece will be the bottom part of his head.

5. Balance the other side of the tomato on top to make a goofy grin. Use a toothpick to poke eyeholes in the tomato head and press in the currants for eyes. Poke 2 more holes on top of the head and push in the carrot sticks for the antennae.

6. Enjoy your hungry caterpillar before he turns into a butterfly!

A NOVEL IDEA

Instead of serving dinner in courses, serve it in chapters. Take turns making up a story for each chapter. See how silly your story gets!

Take a bite out of these food-themed books:

Harry Hungry!
by Steven Salerno

Pinkalicious
by Victoria Kann and Elizabeth Kann

Fussy Freya
by Katharine Quarmby and Piet Grobler

Little Pea
by Amy Krouse Rosenthal and Jen Corace

How Are You Peeling?
by Saxton Freymann and Joost Elffers

Would you rather eat green eggs and ham or stone soup?

With which book character would you like to trade places for the day?

If you were the hungry caterpillar, what is the last food you would eat before building your cocoon?

BAKE BELIEVE

Before you start baking, pretend you're
a storybook character. Call yourself that
name the entire time in the kitchen!

144

the three bears

Makes 12 cookies

1	cup Bean Appétit Flour Blend (page xiii)
⅔	cup packed light brown sugar
½	cup quick oats
1	teaspoon baking powder
¼	teaspoon ground cinnamon
	Pinch of salt
6	tablespoons Chickpea Puree (page xiii)
1	teaspoon vanilla extract
4	tablespoons unsalted butter, softened
2	tablespoons water
12	dried figs
12	(¼-inch-thick) banana slices
6	raisins, cut in half
24	mini chocolate chips
24	white chocolate chips

1. Preheat the oven to 350°F.

2. Give your best bear growl as you combine the flour blend, brown sugar, oats, baking powder, cinnamon, and salt in a bowl. Add the pureed chickpeas and vanilla and stir. Mix in the butter, and then slowly add the water.

3. Form the dough into three different size circles, one small size for Baby Bear, one medium size for Mama Bear, and one big size for Papa Bear.

4. Place the bears on a parchment-lined baking tray, and pop them in the oven to bake for 10 to 12 minutes, until golden brown. Let cool.

5. Once the bear cookies have cooled, it's time to add their faces. Cut the figs in half, and place them at the top of each cookie for ears. Place a small banana slice in the center of each bear's face for the nose, and place a raisin half on top of each banana slice. Press the mini chocolate chips into the white chocolate chips for eyes and place 2 eyes above each bear's nose. Grrrreat!

145

HOT CROSS FUN!

How many nursery rhymes can your family think of that mention food? (Hint: Think of "tuffets," and "Peter, Peter.")

If you scored:

Less than 3: Easy as Pie!

3–6: Cool as a Cucumber!

7 or more: Take the Cake!

refined bean

A-B-C-D-EAT!

Wait until everyone at the dinner table has his food before eating. See how many times you can sing the ABC's until everyone's served!

Place some branches in a vase filled with rocks or marbles.

Write something nice you can do for someone (wash dishes, fold laundry, help with homework) on little pieces of paper. Punch holes in the top and use ribbon to hang the papers on your Giving Tree branches.

When you're feeling extra kind, pick a tag off the tree and give that person your gift of helping!

THE GIVING TREE

green bean

writings on the wall

Do you have books that are tattered and torn, but you can't bear to throw them away? Use salvaged pages to decorate anything from a tabletop to a playhouse wall.

YOU WILL NEED:

Sponge brush

Decoupage glue (like Mod Podge)

Book pages

Using the sponge brush, spread a thin layer of decoupage glue onto the surface you want to decorate. Place a book page on the surface and coat with another thin layer of glue. Repeat this step, overlapping the book pages slightly so none of the original surface is visible.

Make sure to smooth out any bubbles on the pages by pressing firmly with the sponge brush. Once the surface is completely covered, apply a final thin coat of the decoupage glue and let dry.

tasty tales

Make up your own fairy tale. You must use the following cooking terms in your story:

Boil   Cup   Preheat   Mix   Sprinkle

After completing the challenge, cut out the Peanocchio square on page 193 and attach it to your *Bean Appétit* diploma!

pea-nochle

EDIBLE GAME NIGHT

EAT YOUR WORDS

This silly version of Scrabble is smart and scrumptious! You will need:

- **Checkered tablecloth**

- **1 box alphabet-shaped cereal**

- **1 bowl per person**

- **Paper and pencil**

Place the tablecloth on the table or floor. Each player reaches in the cereal box and pulls out 12 letters. Hide the letters in your bowl, so no one else can see them.

The first player uses two or more letters from his bowl to form a word, placing one letter in each square on the table-cloth to read either across or down. One point is earned for each letter used in the word. Then that player draws as many new letters from the cereal box as he played; always keep 12 letters in your bowl, as long as there are enough letters left in the cereal box.

The next player adds one or more letters to those already played to form a new word. One point is earned for each letter used in the new word.

The first player to reach 25 points wins. Celebrate the fun with bowls of yummy cereal!

TASTY
TONGUE TWISTERS

Who can say all 3 funny food sayings first
without getting tongue-tied?

Chocolate chip cookies in a
copper coffee cup.

Miss Smith's fish-
sauce shop seldom
sells shellfish.

A box of mixed
biscuits and a
biscuit mixer.

black-eyed pea

FAMILY FOOD FIGHT

Each family member searches the kitchen for 3 ingredients each, from ground turkey to peanut butter to cinnamon. Bring your ingredients back to the table and place them in front of your seat.

Each player has 30 minutes to create a dish using at least 1 ingredient from each person. After all the dishes are prepared, take turns taste-testing each meal. Vote on the tastiest!

Follow up your family food fight with a game of Delicious Dominoes (page 156)!

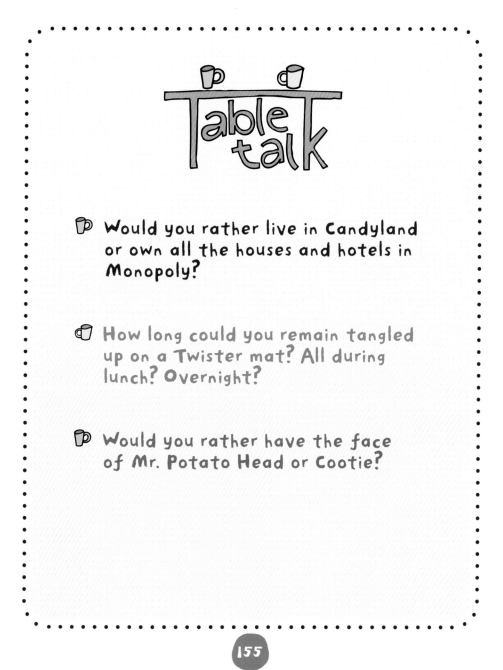

Table talk

🍵 Would you rather live in Candyland or own all the houses and hotels in Monopoly?

🍵 How long could you remain tangled up on a Twister mat? All during lunch? Overnight?

🍵 Would you rather have the face of Mr. Potato Head or Cootie?

delicious dominoes!

Serves 4

1   **cup Bean Appétit Flour Blend (page xiii)**

¼   **cup cocoa powder**

½   **cup plus 2 tablespoons packed light brown sugar**

½   **teaspoon baking soda**

     Pinch of ground cinnamon

3   **tablespoons butter, softened**

1   **tablespoon honey**

2   **tablespoons water**

1   **teaspoon vanilla extract**

¼   **cup lowfat cream cheese**

     Bag of white chocolate chips

YOU WILL ALSO NEED:
Piping bag

1. Before making the dough, have your family line up in a line. Pretend to fall like a stack of dominoes. Now you're ready to cook!

2. Preheat the oven to 350°F and lightly spray a baking sheet with nonstick spray.

3. Count by ones as you combine the flour blend, cocoa powder, brown sugar, baking soda, and cinnamon in a bowl. Add the butter and stir until combined. Add the honey, water, and vanilla and mix until the dough is sticky. Press the dough flat on a parchment-lined baking tray. Chill in the freezer for 5 minutes.

4. Count by twos as you roll out the dough to ¼ inch thick. Use a butter knife to make 1 by 2-inch rectangles.

5. Place the rectangles on the prepared baking sheet and bake for 12 to 15 minutes, or until golden brown. Remove the cookies from the oven and let them cool for 5 minutes.

6. While the cookies are cooling, place the cream cheese in a piping bag. Once your cookies have cooled, use the piping bag of cream cheese to draw a horizontal line through the halfway point of your domino. Dab a little bit of cream cheese on the bottom of the white chocolate chips. Then add the white chocolate chips on both sides of the line to form the white dots on the dominoes, alternating numbers 1 to 6.

7. Kick off your family dessert with a game of Delicious Dominoes. The winner gets to devour the dominoes first!

DUST BUSTERS

Each player gets 1 minute to choose how to move around the house cleaning up after dinner—from hopping on your right foot to slithering like a snake. Rotate turns until the house is clean!

GAME ON!

Try using food to create your own edible versions of your family's favorite games!

- Stack carrots to play your own version of Jenga.

- Use zucchini circles and crisscrossed snow peas for a crunchy competition of tic-tac-toe.

- Your fingers will get frosty when you use frozen peas for a marbles match!

BEAN-NANZA!

For 2 players

Give each player a pile of dried beans and a cup.

For each round, secretly choose either 1, 2, or 3 beans to put under your own cup. On the count of "1, 2, Pea!," lift up your cup to reveal how many beans you set out.

One bean beats 2, 2 beats 3, and 3 beats 1. The winner keeps her beans and collects the other person's as well. (Ties go back to the owners.) Play until one person has the whole pile!

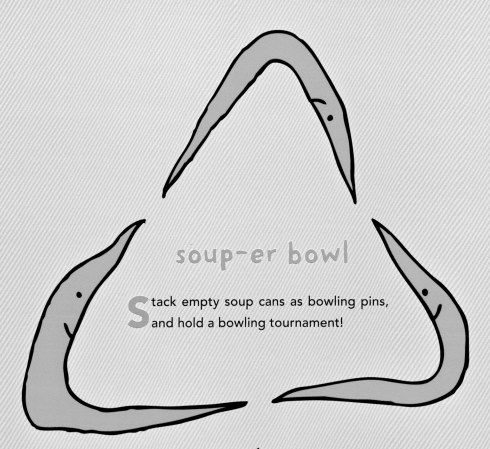

soup-er bowl

Stack empty soup cans as bowling pins, and hold a bowling tournament!

green bean

pea brain

In what game can you find Spare Ribs, Bread Basket, and Adam's Apple?

Answer: Operation. Cavity Sam also has a Growling Stomach!

how do you peel?

Try peeling an orange in 1 big piece. Can you do it in 5 pieces or fewer? If so, you win the challenge!

After completing the challenge, cut out the Pea-nochle square on page 193 and attach it to your *Bean Appétit* diploma.

sweet pea

DELICIOUS DESSERTS

SMART COOKIE!

10 things to do with a cookie cutter (besides making cookies!):

1. Dunk into bubble mix and blow odd-shaped bubbles.

2. Make designer pancakes. Spray cooking spray on the inside of a metal cookie cutter and place it on a hot griddle or a skillet. Then pour the pancake batter into the cookie cutter. When the pancake sets, remove the cookie cutter and finish cooking the pancake.

3. Place in planting pots and grow grass in crazy shapes!

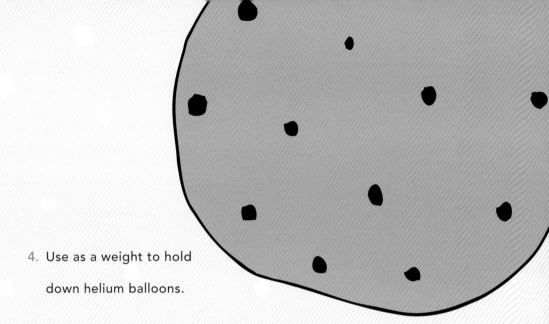

4. Use as a weight to hold down helium balloons.

5. Hang several metal cookie cutters together to make your own wind chime.

6. Use as a stencil for a wall mural.

7. Cut fun cheese slice shapes to spruce up cheese and crackers.

8. Trace around and cut out felt drink coasters.

9. Use it at the beach to decorate your sand castle.

10. String it on a piece of ribbon and wear around your neck—it's a good conversation piece!

cookie cones

Makes 4 cones

⅓ **stick unsalted butter, softened**

¼ **cup packed light brown sugar**

2 **tablespoons Chickpea Puree (page xiii)**

Pinch of salt

¼ **teaspoon vanilla extract**

½ **cup Bean Appétit Flour Blend (page xiii)**

Natural food coloring (available at natural food stores)

Frosting (page 173)

4 **ice cream cones**

Sprinkles

YOU WILL ALSO NEED:
Tiny cookie cutters

1. Preheat the oven to 350°F.

2. Before you begin, say something sweet to each other. In a large bowl, use an electric mixer to beat the butter, brown sugar, Chickpea Puree, and salt until light and fluffy. Add the vanilla and mix.

3. With the mixer on low, yell, "Flour power!" as you add the flour blend, and mix just until all the ingredients are combined.

4. Divide the dough between 2 bowls. In one bowl, add a few drops of 1 food coloring. In the other, add a few drops of another food coloring. Stir until the doughs are the colors you like.

5. Wrap both doughs separately in plastic, and chill in the freezer for 10 minutes.

6. While your cookie dough is chilling out, use a butter knife to frost the edges of the ice cream cones, to about ½ inch down from the rim. Coat the frosting with the sprinkles. Set the cones aside.

 8. Place the cookie shapes on a greased cookie sheet and bake for 5 to 7 minutes, until they're slightly firm. Let cool.

7. After your dough is firm, use a rolling pin to roll it to a ⅛-inch thickness. Use the tiny cookie cutters to create fun shapes.

9. Place your cookies in the cones, as many as you can heap in. No need to worry about them melting!

SWEET SIPPERS

Why limit a dessert to something you can eat off a plate? Try these favorite desserts in drink form! Just blend the following ingredients:

pumpkin pie

pureed pumpkin + **pinch of cinnamon**

+ vanilla frozen yogurt

strawberry cheesecake

frozen strawberries + lowfat cream cheese

+ milk + **crushed graham crackers**

carrot cake

carrot juice + **nutmeg** + **cinnamon**

+ frozen pineapple + vanilla yogurt

banana split

banana + **frozen strawberries**

+ frozen pineapple + milk

Drizzle with chocolate syrup and a cherry!

CRAZY CONES

What ice cream flavors do you like on your cone? Check out these unusual flavors from around the globe:

octopus

ox tongue

fried eggplant

corn

cactus

seaweed

lettuce

MUFFIN TIN WIN!

Take turns throwing Ping-Pong balls into a muffin tin. Get a point for every ball that lands in the tin and get **5** points if the ball lands in a corner!

cherry pie pops

Makes 6

½ **cup Bean Appétit Flour Blend (page xiii)**

3 **tablespoons butter, softened**

2 **tablespoons packed brown sugar**

3½ **tablespoons water**

1 **(12-ounce) can organic cherry pie filling**

1 **egg, lightly beaten**

YOU WILL ALSO NEED:
Lollipop sticks

1. Pick your Pied Piper and follow him around the kitchen with a mixing spoon in hand. In a mixing bowl combine the flour blend, butter, and brown sugar. Slowly add water until you can form the dough into a ball. Chill the dough in the freezer for 5 minutes.

2. Preheat the oven to 375° and lightly spray a baking sheet with nonstick spray.

3. Roll the chilled dough onto a lightly floured surface to ¼ inch thick. Use the top of a small cup as a cookie cutter to shape 1½-inch circles. Place a small spoonful of the cherry filling on the center of 1 circle, leaving the outer edges clear. Place another circle of dough on top, slide a lollipop stick in between the 2 dough pieces, and gently press all around the edges of the dough to seal in the filling.

4. Place the lollipops on the prepared baking sheet. Brush the crust with the beaten egg. Bake for 15 to 17 minutes, until the lollipops are golden brown. Hold your arms above your head in a circle so you look like a lollipop before eating away!

reach for the stars!

Makes 4

CAKE

2½ cups Bean Appétit Flour Blend (page xiii)

2¼ cups packed light brown sugar

½ teaspoon ground cinnamon

2¼ teaspoons baking powder

6 tablespoons olive oil

2½ teaspoons vanilla extract

2 tablespoons white vinegar

½ cup Chickpea Puree (page xiii)

1¼ cups water

FROSTING

1 cup lowfat cream cheese

½ cup confectioners' sugar

2 tablespoons packed light brown sugar

1 teaspoon vanilla extract

¼ teaspoon ground cinnamon

3 tablespoons milk

Star-shaped cake-decorating sprinkles

YOU WILL ALSO NEED:

Jumbo muffin liners (available at craft stores)

Regular muffin liners

Mini muffin liners (available at craft stores)

4 small stickers, photos, or other images cut in a star shape

4 toothpicks

1. Preheat the oven to 350°F. Line a muffin pan with 4 jumbo and regular muffin liners. Line a mini muffin pan with 4 mini liners.

2. Stand on your tiptoes and reach for the stars before combining the flour blend, brown sugar, cinnamon, and baking powder in a large bowl. Stir in the olive oil, vanilla, and vinegar. Fold in the Chickpea Puree. Slowly add the water and stir until smooth.

3. Divide the batter among the muffin liners so you have 4 of each size. Bake the mini cupcakes for 12 to 14 minutes, the medium cupcakes for 16 to 18 minutes, and the jumbo cupcakes for 25 to 30 minutes. Let cool.

4. Make a wish on a star while you make the frosting. Use an electric mixer to mix the cream cheese, confectioners' sugar, brown sugar, vanilla, and cinnamon. Add the milk and beat until fluffy.

5. Frost all the cupcakes and decorate with sprinkles. Stack a medium cupcake on top of a large cupcake. Add a small cupcake to the top of the medium cupcake to create your sweet stack.

6. Top each tower with a star picture taped to a toothpick. You go, superstar!

pea brain

In some European countries, kids call cupcakes *fairy cakes*!

Table Talk

- Would you rather have a house painted in frosting or a chimney made of brownie bricks?

- If you owned a cupcake factory, what friend or family member would you hire to be your chief taste-tester?

- Out of everyone in your family, who is least likely to steal a cookie from the cookie jar?

Cookie Jar

press play

Practice using a garlic press, pressing 3 different foods. You can press bananas for muffins or bread. Or you can put a small ball of dough in the press and form long strands that can be used as "hair" for decorating cookie girls and boys!

After completing the challenge, cut out the Sweet Pea square on page 193 and attach it to your *Bean Appétit* diploma!

metric and conversion charts

TO CONVERT	MULTIPLY
Ounces to grams	Ounces by 28.35
Pounds to kilograms	Pounds by .454
Teaspoons to milliliters	Teaspoons by 4.93
Tablespoons to milliliters	Tablespoons by 14.79
Fluid ounces to milliliters	Fluid ounces by 29.57
Cups to milliliters	Cups by 236.59
Cups to liters	Cups by .236
Pints to liters	Pints by .473
Quarts to liters	Quarts by .946
Gallons to liters	Gallons by 3.785
Inches to centimeters	Inches by 2.54

APPROXIMATE METRIC EQUIVALENTS

WEIGHT

¼ ounce	7 grams	3 ounces	.85 grams
½ ounce	.14 grams	4 ounces (¼ pound)	113 grams
¾ ounce	.21 grams	5 ounces	142 grams
1 ounce	.28 grams	6 ounces	170 grams
1¼ ounces	.35 grams	7 ounces	198 grams
1½ ounces	42.5 grams	8 ounces (½ pound)	227 grams
1⅔ ounces	.45 grams	16 ounces (1 pound)	454 grams
2 ounces	.57 grams	35.25 ounces (2.2 pounds)	1 kilogram

VOLUME

¼ teaspoon	1 milliliter
½ teaspoon	2.5 milliliters
¾ teaspoon	4 milliliters
1 teaspoon	5 milliliters
1¼ teaspoons	6 milliliters
1½ teaspoons	7.5 milliliters
1¾ teaspoons	8.5 milliliters
2 teaspoons	10 milliliters
1 tablespoon (½ fluid ounce)	15 milliliters
2 tablespoons (1 fluid ounce)	30 milliliters
¼ cup	60 milliliters
⅓ cup	80 milliliters
½ cup (4 fluid ounces)	120 milliliters
⅔ cup	160 milliliters
¾ cup	180 milliliters
1 cup (8 fluid ounces)	240 milliliters
1¼ cups	300 milliliters
1½ cups (12 fluid ounces)	360 milliliters
1⅔ cups	400 milliliters
2 cups (1 pint)	460 milliliters
3 cups	700 milliliters
4 cups (1 quart)	0.95 liter
1 quart plus ¼ cup	1 liter
4 quarts (1 gallon)	3.8 liters

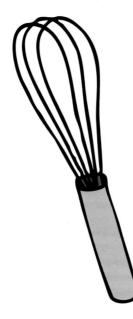

LENGTH

⅛ inch	3 millimeters
¼ inch	6 millimeters
½ inch	1¼ centimeters
1 inch	2½ centimeters
2 inches	5 centimeters
2½ inches	6 centimeters
4 inches	10 centimeters
5 inches	13 centimeters
6 inches	15¼ centimeters
12 inches (1 foot)	30 centimeters

METRIC AND CONVERSION CHARTS

COMMON INGREDIENTS AND THEIR APPROXIMATE EQUIVALENTS

1 cup uncooked white rice = 185 grams

1 cup all-purpose flour = 140 grams

1 stick butter (4 ounces • ½ cup • 8 tablespoons) = 110 grams

1 cup butter (8 ounces • 2 sticks • 16 tablespoons) = 220 grams

1 cup brown sugar, firmly packed = 225 grams

1 cup granulated sugar = 200 grams

OVEN TEMPERATURES

To convert Fahrenheit to Celsius, subtract 32 from Fahrenheit, multiply the result by 5, then divide by 9.

DESCRIPTION	FAHRENHEIT	CELSIUS	BRITISH GAS MARK
Very cool	200°	95°	0
Very cool	225°	110°	¼
Very cool	250°	120°	½
Cool	275°	135°	1
Cool	300°	150°	2
Warm	325°	165°	3
Moderate	350°	175°	4
Moderately hot	375°	190°	5
Fairly hot	400°	200°	6
Hot	425°	220°	7
Very hot	450°	230°	8
Very hot	475°	245°	9

Information compiled from a variety of sources, including *Recipes into Type* by Joan Whitman and Dolores Simon (Newton, MA: Biscuit Books, 2000); *The New Food Lover's Companion* by Sharon Tyler Herbst (Hauppauge, NY: Barron's, 1995); and *Rosemary Brown's Big Kitchen Instruction Book* (Kansas City, MO: Andrews McMeel, 1998).

index

INDEX

INDEX

INDEX

for more yummy,
good-for-you recipes
and food fun, visit:

www.beansproutscafe.com

become a star chef with our chef challenge!

Each chapter of *Bean Appétit* contains a different challenge.

When you complete each challenge, cut out the square on

page 193 and attach it to your *Bean Appétit* diploma, which

you can download at www.beansproutscafe.com!